flag Sticker Atlas

picthall and gunzi

Europe

Europe is the fifth-largest continent in the world. It contains 45 countries. More than 730 million people live in Europe, speaking many different languages. The biggest country in the world is Russia. Part of Russia is in Europe and the rest of Russia is in Asia. Europe also contains the smallest country in the world, which is the Vatican City!

Biggest country

The biggest country in Europe is Russia. Large areas are covered in forest. People use planes to deliver things to each other!

Smallest country

The Vatican City is the tiniest country in Europe. It is inside Italy, and it contains St Peter's Basilica and the Apostolic Palace, where the Pope lives.

Biggest city

Moscow is Europe's biggest city. It is also the seventh-largest city in the world and is a mega city. Mega cities have a population with over 10 million people.

THE WOW!

Europe is named after Princess Europa, from Greek mythology. She was so beautiful that Zeus, the king of the gods, fell in love with her.

FACTOR

ABOUT EUROPE

Number of countries	45
Size	World's 5th-largest continent
Total area	10,531,000 sq kilometres (including the Asian part of Russia)
Population	738 million people
Biggest country	Russia – 17,098,242 square kilometres
Smallest country	Vatican City – total area 440,000 square metres
Biggest city	Moscow, Russia

Country-by-country facts

There are 45 countries in Europe and more than 230 languages. The two languages used most often are English and German. There are more than 20 different sorts of currency, and 23 countries are using the euro. You can see all of Europe's flags on these pages.

Iceland
Capital City Reykjavik
Population 311,058
Area 103,000 sq km
Main languages Icelandic

Norway
Capital City Oslo
Population 4,691,849
Area 323,802 sq km
Main languages Norwegian

Denmark
Capital City Copenhagen
Population 5,529,888
Area 43,094 sq km
Main languages Danish

Sweden
Capital City Stockholm
Population 9,088,728
Area 450,295 sq km
Main languages Swedish

Finland
Capital City Helsinki
Population 5,259,250
Area 338,145 sq km
Main languages Finnish and Swedish

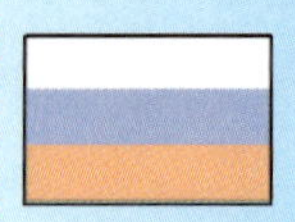

Russia
Capital City Moscow
Population 138,739,892
Area 17,098,242 sq km
Main languages Russian

Belarus
Capital City Minsk
Population 9,577,552
Area 207,600 sq km
Main languages Belarusian and Russian

Ireland
Capital City Dublin
Population 4,670,976
Area 70,273 sq km
Main languages English and Irish

United Kingdom
Capital City London
Population 62,698,362
Area 243,610 sq km
Main languages English, Welsh

Netherlands
Capital Cities Amsterdam and The Hague
Population 16,847,007
Area 41,543 sq km
Main languages Dutch

Belgium
Capital City Brussels
Population 10,431,477
Area 30,528 sq km
Main languages Dutch, French and German

Luxembourg
Capital City Luxembourg
Population 503,302
Area 2,586 sq km
Main languages German, French and Luxembourgish

Visit London!

The capital of the United Kingdom is London. This is the most visited city in the world. London is famous for its theatres, museums, art, business and fashion. One of London's famous sights is this giant wheel, called the London Eye.

Germany
Capital City Berlin
Population 81,471,834
Area 357,022 sq km
Main languages German

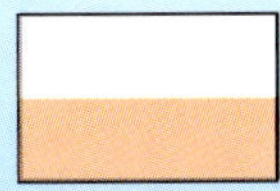

Poland
Capital City Warsaw
Population 38,441,588
Area 312,685 sq km
Main languages Polish

Lithuania
Capital City Vilnius
Population 3,535,547
Area 65,300 sq km
Main languages Lithuanian,
Polish and Russian

Latvia
Capital City Riga
Population 2,204,708
Area 64,589 sq km
Main languages Latvian
and Russian

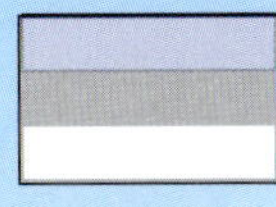

Estonia
Capital City Tallinn
Population 1,282,963
Area 45,228 sq km
Main languages Estonian
and Russian

France

France
Capital City Paris
Population 65,312,249
Area 643,427 sq km
Main languages French

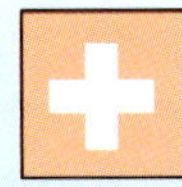

Switzerland
Capital City Bern
Population 7,639,961
Area 41,277 sq km
Main languages German,
French, Italian and Romansch

Liechtenstein
Capital City Vaduz
Population 35,236
Area 160 sq km
Main languages German
and Alemannic

Austria
Capital City Vienna
Population 8,217,280
Area 83,871 sq km
Main languages German

Czech Republic
Capital City Prague
Population 10,190,213
Area 78,867 sq km
Main languages Czech

Hungary
Capital City Budapest
Population 9,976,062
Area 93,028 sq km
Main languages Hungarian

The Grand Duchy
Luxembourg is one of the smallest countries
in the world, and one of the richest in Europe.
The official name for Luxembourg is the Grand
Duchy of Luxembourg. It is ruled by a Grand Duke
and is the only Grand Duchy in the world!

Slovakia
Capital City Bratislava
Population 5,477,038
Area 49,035 sq km
Main languages Slovak

Romania
Capital City Bucharest
Population 21,904,551
Area 238,391 sq km
Main languages Romanian

Moldova
Capital City Chisinau
Population 4,314,377
Area 33,851 sq km
Main languages Moldovan,
Russian and Gagauz

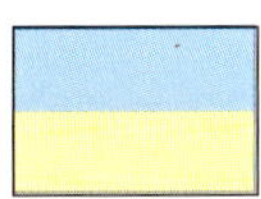

Ukraine
Capital City Kiev
Population 45,134,707
Area 603,550 sq km
Main languages Ukranian
and Russian

Small and wealthy

The rich country of Monaco is so tiny that you can walk from one side of it to the other side in half an hour, but this is also Europe's most crowded country. More people live here per square kilometre than anywhere else in Europe.

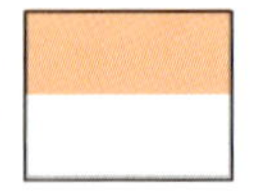

Monaco
Capital City Monaco-Ville
Population 30,539
Area 2 sq km
Main languages French

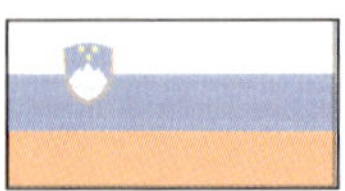

Slovenia
Capital City Ljubljana
Population 2,000,092
Area 20,273 sq km
Main languages Slovenian

Serbia
Capital City Belgrade
Population 7,310,555
Area 77,474 sq km
Main languages Serbian
into smaller units.)

San Marino
Capital City San Marino
Population 31,817
Area 61 sq km
Main languages Italian

Croatia
Capital City Zagreb
Population 4,483,804
Area 56,594 sq km
Main languages Croatian

Kosovo
Capital City Pristina
Population 1,825,632
Area 10,887 sq km
Main languages Albanian, Serbian

Vatican City
Capital City Vatican City
Population 832
Area 0.44 sq km
Main languages Italian

Bosnia and Herzegovina
Capital City Sarajevo
Population 4,622,163

Area 51,197 sq km
Main languages Bosnian, Serbian,Croatian

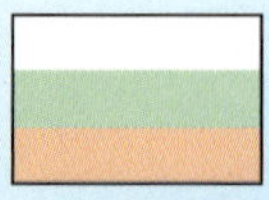

Bulgaria
Capital City Sofia
Population 7,093,635
Area 110,879 sq km
Main languages Bulgarian

Andorra
Capital City Andorra La Vella
Population 84,825
Area 468 sq km
Main languages Spanish, French, Portuguese

Montenegro
Capital City Podgorica
Population 661,807
Area 13,812
Main languages Serbian, Montenegrin

Newest capital city

Europe's newest capital is Pristina, in Kosovo. Its National Library is an amazing building covered in a big metal net. It represents the brain and learning.

Macedonia
Capital City Skopje
Population 2,077,328
Area 25,713
Main languages Macedonian

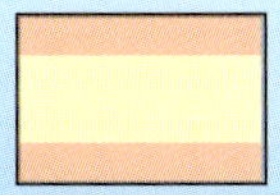

Spain
Capital City Madrid
Population 46,754,784
Area 505,370 sq km
Main languages Spanish, Catalan, Galician, Basque

Italy
Capital City Rome
Population 61,016,804
Area 301,340 sq km
Main languages Italian

Albania
Capital City Tirana
Population 2,994,667
Area 28,748 sq km
Main languages Albanian

Portugal
Capital City Lisbon
Population 10,760,305
Area 92,090 sq km
Main languages Portuguese, Mirandese

Malta
Capital City Valletta
Population 408,333
Area 316 sq km
Main languages Maltese, English

Greece
Capital City Athens
Population 10,760,136
Area 131,957 sq km
Main languages Greek

Where are you from?

Here are some of the European national car stickers. Everyone who drives their car outside their own country has to put a sticker on the back bumper of the car. Or, they must have a number plate that shows which country they are from.

ABOUT THE COINS

The fronts of all the euro coins are the same for every country that uses the euro. This is the front of a two euro coin.

The designs on the backs of euro coins are usually different for each country. Here are the backs of the two euro coins from six countries in Europe.

TELL US ABOUT THE EURO!

Euro coins are designed so that people can recognise which coins they have just by touching them. Each euro coin is a different size and weight and each has a special, and different, edge.

Two, ten and twenty euro cents

Germany

France

Malta

Italy

Netherlands

Cyprus

Asia

This is the world's biggest continent, with 48 countries. The largest country is Russia, then China. The smallest is the Republic of Maldives. More people live in Asia than in any other continent. There are over 1,500 languages and lots of religions and cultures.

Biggest city

Mumbai, in India, is the biggest city in Asia. This 'mega city' is home to over 14 million people. They earn much more here than people in the rest of India.

Smallest country

Asia's smallest country is made up of a group of beautiful islands in the Indian Ocean. They are called the Maldives. These tiny islands are actually the tops of a gigantic underwater mountain range!

List of Abbreviations

U.A.E. United Arab Emirates

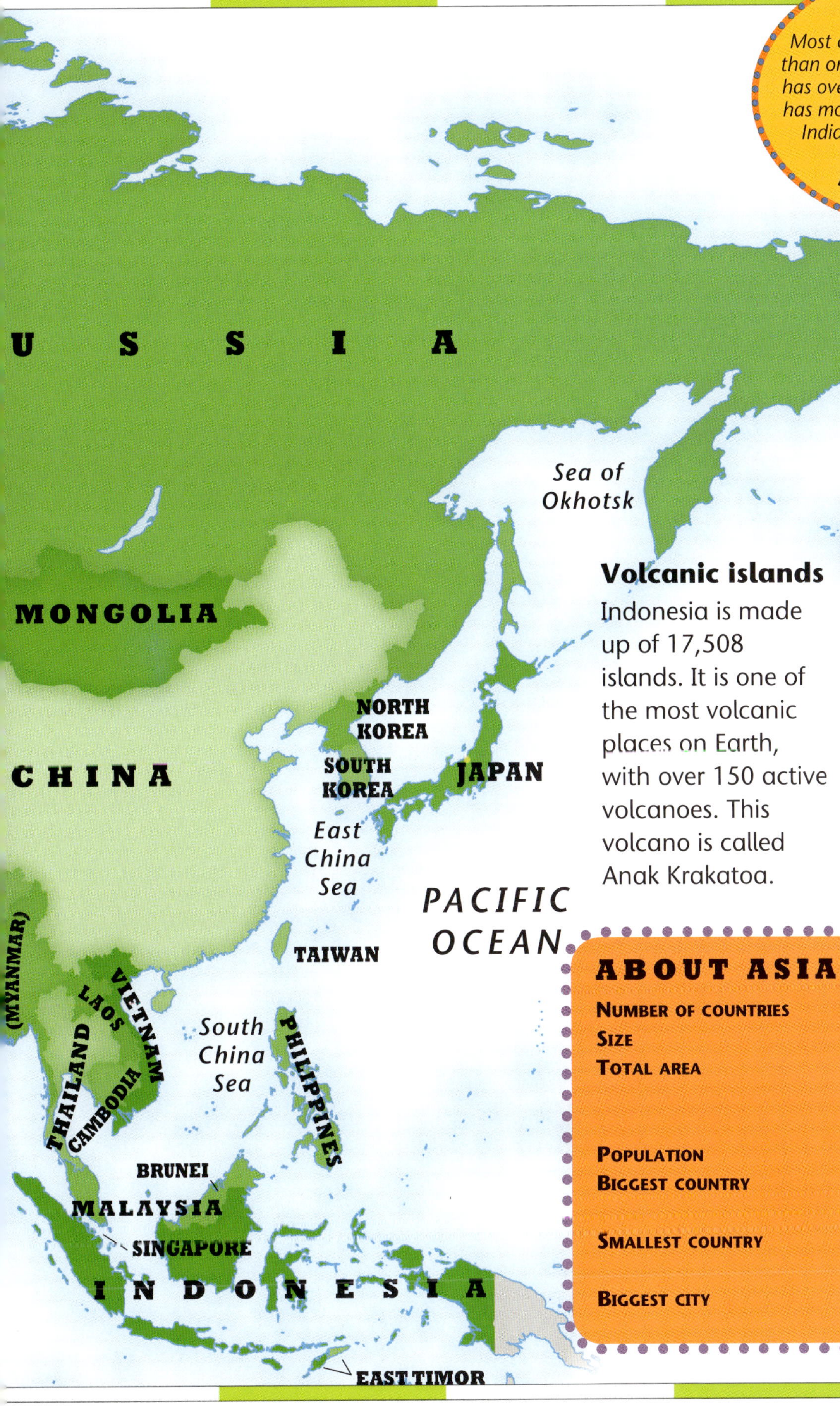

THE WOW! FACTOR

Most countries in Asia have more than one language. The Philippines has over 100 languages, Indonesia has more than 600 languages and India has over 800 languages!

Volcanic islands

Indonesia is made up of 17,508 islands. It is one of the most volcanic places on Earth, with over 150 active volcanoes. This volcano is called Anak Krakatoa.

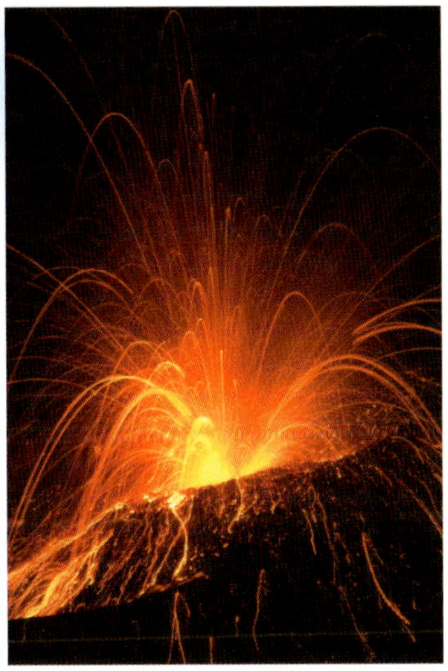

ABOUT ASIA

Number of countries	48
Size	World's largest continent
Total area	44,579,000 sq kilometres (including the Asian part of Russia)
Population	4.1 billion people
Biggest country	Russia – 17,098,242 square kilometres
Smallest country	Maldives – total area 298 square kilometres
Biggest city	Mumbai (Bombay), India

Country-by-country facts

There are 48 countries in Asia and more than 1,500 languages are spoken here. Chinese Mandarin, Hindi, Bengali and English are the most widely used languages. There are 48 currencies being used in Asia, including the euro and the US dollar.

Kazakhstan
Capital City Astana
Population 15,522,373
Area 2,724,900 sq km
Main languages Kazakh, Russian

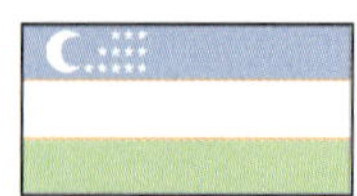

Uzbekistan
Capital City Tashkent (Toshkent)
Population 28,128,600
Area 447,400 sq km
Main languages Uzbek, Russian, Tajik

Cyprus
Capital City Nicosia (Lefkosia)
Population 1,120,489
Area 9,251 sq km
Main languages Greek, Turkish

Turkey
Capital City Ankara
Population 78,785,548
Area 783,562 sq km
Main languages Turkish

Georgia
Capital City T'bilisi
Population 4,585,874
Area 69,700 sq km
Main languages Georgian

Kyrgyzstan
Capital City Bishkek
Population 5,587,443
Area 199,951 sq km
Main languages Kyrgyz, Russian

Lebanon
Capital City Beirut
Population 4,143,101
Area 10,400 sq km
Main languages Arabic

Syria
Capital City Damascus
Population 22,517,750
Area 185,180 sq km
Main languages Arabic

Holy city

The capital city of Israel is Jerusalem. For the three major religions – Judaism, Islam and Christianity – this is the holiest city in the world. Many people believe that it is the place where both Mohammed and Jesus rose into Heaven.

Armenia
Capital City Yerevan
Population 2,967,975
Area 29,743 sq km
Main languages Armenian, Russian

Turkmenistan
Capital City Ashgabat (Ashkhabad)
Population 4,997,503
Area 488,100 sq km
Main languages Turkmen, Russian

Israel
Capital City Jerusalem
Population 7,473,052
Area 22,072 sq km
Main languages Hebrew, Arabic

Iraq
Capital City Baghdad
Population 30,399,572
Area 438,317 sq km
Main languages Arabic, Kurdish

Room to roam

The country of Mongolia is enormous but very few people live here. There are only about three million people living in the whole country. There is hardly any farmland, and large areas of the country are covered by mountains, grassy plains called steppes, and the Gobi – a big, cold desert.

Azerbaijan
Capital City Baku (Baki, Baky)
Population 8,372,373
Area 86,600 sq km
Main languages Azeri, Russian

Tajikistan
Capital City Dushanbe
Population 7,627,200
Area 143,100 sq km
Main languages Tajik, Uzbek, Russian

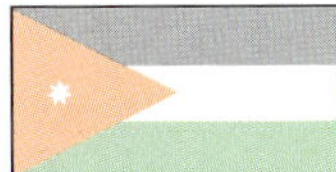

Jordan
Capital City Amman
Population 6,508,271
Area 89,342 sq km
Main languages Arabic

Kuwait
Capital City Kuwait City
Population 2,595,628
Area 17,818 sq km
Main languages Arabic

Iran
Capital City Tehran
Population 77,891,220
Area 1,648,195 sq km
Main languages Persian

Afghanistan
Capital City Kabul
Population 29,835,392
Area 652,230 sq km
Main languages Pashto, Dari (Persian)

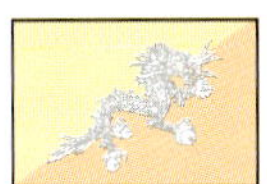

Bhutan
Capital City Thimphu
Population 708,427
Area 38,394 sq km
Main languages Dzongkha

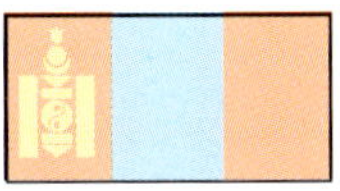

Mongolia
Capital City Ulaanbaatar
Population 3,133,318
Area 1,564,116 sq km
Main languages Mongolian

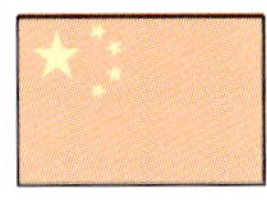

China
Capital City Beijing
Population 1,336,718,015
Area 9,596,961 sq km
Main languages Mandarin Chinese

MODERN CHINA

After communist Chairman Mao died in 1976 the Chinese government began to allow people to farm, and to buy and sell things for themselves. Now China exports all sorts of things, including toys, clothes, books and computers, to other places in the world. Many countries spend lots of money on Chinese goods. This has made China become a rich and powerful country.

Shanghai is the fastest-growing city in China.

Japan's capital

The richest nation in Asia is Japan. Tokyo is the largest city, and it is the capital of Japan. Japan's government is based in Tokyo, and the Imperial Palace is here, too. This is the home of the Emperor of Japan.

Taiwan
Capital City Taipei
Population 23,071,779
Area 35,980 sq km
Main languages Mandarin Chinese, Min Nan Chinese (Taiwanese)

Japan
Capital City Tokyo
Population 126,475,664
Area 377,915 sq km
Main languages Japanese

North Korea
Capital City Pyongyang
Population 24,457,492
Area 120,538 sq km
Main languages Korean

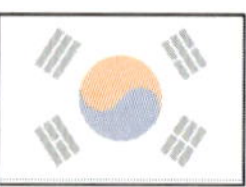

South Korea
Capital City Seoul
Population 48,754,657
Area 99,720 sq km
Main languages Korean

Saudi Arabia
Capital City Riyadh
Population 26,131,703
Area 2,149,690 sq km
Main languages Arabic

Bahrain
Capital City Manama
Population 1,214,705
Area 760 sq km
Main languages Arabic

Pakistan
Capital City Islamabad
Population 187,342,721
Area 796,095 sq km
Main languages English, Urdu, Punjabi, Sindhi, Pashto, Balochi

Nepal
Capital City Kathmandu
Population 29,391,883
Area 147,181 sq km
Main languages Nepali

Burma
Capital City Naypyidaw
Population 54,584,650
Area 676,578 sq km
Main languages Burmese and local languages

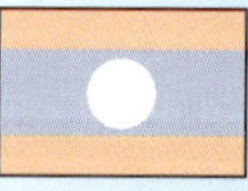

Laos
Capital City Vientiane (Viangchan)
Population 6,477,211
Area 236,800 sq km
Main languages Lao, French

Vietnam
Capital City Hanoi
Population 90,549,390
Area 331,210 sq km
Main languages Vietnamese

Qatar
Capital City Doha
Population 848,016
Area 11,586 sq km
Main languages Arabic

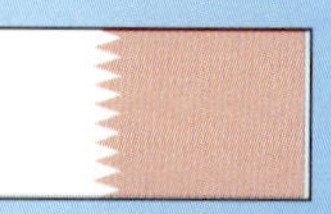

United Arab Emirates
Capital City Abu Dhabi
Population 5,148,664
Area 83,600 sq km
Main languages Arabic

India
Capital City New Delhi
Population 1,189,172,906
Area 3,287,263 sq km
Main languages Hindi, English and at least 16 other official languages

Bangladesh
Capital City Dhaka
Population 158,570,535
Area 143,998 sq km
Main languages Bengali

Thailand
Capital City Bangkok
Population 66,720,153
Area 513,120 sq km
Main languages Thai

Cambodia
Capital City Phnom Penh
Population 14,701,717
Area 181,035 sq km
Main languages Khmer

Brunei
Capital City Bandar Seri Begawan
Population 401,890
Area 5,765 sq km
Main languages Malay, English, Chinese

Philippines
Capital City Manila
Population 101,833,938
Area 300,000 sq km
Main languages Filipino, English

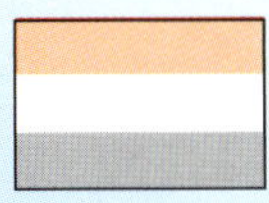

Yemen
Capital City Sanaa
Population 24,133,492
Area 527,968 sq km
Main languages Arabic

Oman
Capital City Muscat
Population 3,027,959
Area 309,500 sq km
Main languages Arabic

Maldives
Capital City Male
Population 394,999
Area 298 sq km
Main languages Divehi
Money 1 rufiyaa = 100 laari

SINGAPORE

This tiny country is made up of 65 islands. It is one of the smallest countries in the world, and it is also known as a 'city-state'. Singapore is one of Asia's busiest ports and it is important for building and repairing ships. Singapore has a huge oil refinery too.

Sri Lanka
Capital City Colombo
Population 21,481,334
Area 65,610 sq km
Main languages Sinhala, Tamil, English

Malaysia
Capital City Kuala Lumpur
Population 28,728,607
Area 329,847 sq km
Main languages Malay, English, Chinese dialects, Tamil, Telugu, Malayalam

Singapore
Capital City Singapore
Population 4,740,737
Area 697 sq km
Main languages English, Malay, Mandarin, Tamil

Indonesia
Capital City Jakarta
Population 245,613,043
Area 1,904,569 sq km
Main languages Indonesian and 300 local languages

East Timor
Capital City Dili
Population 1,177,834
Area 14,874 sq km
Main languages Tetum, Portuguese, Indonesian, English

Tea in Sri Lanka

This country is the fourth biggest tea producer in the world. The tea grows on plantations in the highlands. Then it is sold around the world.

North America

This is the third-largest continent in the world, with 23 countries. It stretches from Greenland, where it is freezing, to the Caribbean, where it is hot. The first people came here from Asia 20,000 years ago. About 500 years ago people from Europe, Africa and Asia started to arrive, with their new languages and religions.

Biggest country

Canada is North America's biggest country. Its border with the United States is the longest in the world. The huge Niagara Falls form part of this border. This enormous waterfall is in Canada and in the United States too!

Biggest city

More people live in Mexico City than any other city in North America. There are over 20 million people in this lively place!

ABOUT NORTH AMERICA

NUMBER OF COUNTRIES	23
SIZE	World's 3rd-largest continent
TOTAL AREA	24,709,000 sq kilometres
POPULATION	529 million people
BIGGEST COUNTRY	Canada – 9,984,670 square kilometres
SMALLEST COUNTRY	St Kitts and Nevis – total area 261 square kilometres
BIGGEST CITY	Mexico City, Mexico

THE WOW!

The border between Mexico and The United States of America is the busiest border in the world! More than 250 million people cross this border every year.

FACTOR

Smallest country

The islands of St Kitts and Nevis make up the smallest nation in North America. They have the smallest land area and the tiniest population!

Country-by-country facts

There are 23 countries in North America and more than 200 different languages. Most of the people living here speak English, Spanish or French. There are more than 17 different kinds of currency being used in North America.

Canada
Capital City Ottawa
Population 34,030,589
Area 9,984,670 sq km
Main languages English, French

United States of America
Capital City Washington DC
Population 313,232,044
Area 9,826,675 sq km
Main languages English

Mexico
Capital City Mexico City (Distrito Federal)
Population 113,724,226
Area 1,964,375 sq km
Main languages Spanish

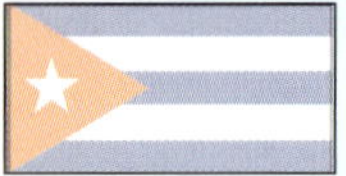

Cuba
Capital City Havana
Population 11,087,330
Area 110,860 sq km
Main languages Spanish

Bahamas
Capital City Nassau
Population 313,312
Area 13,880 sq km
Main languages English

Guatemala
Capital City Guatemala City
Population 13,824,463
Area 108,889 sq km
Main languages Spanish and more than 20 local languages

Belize
Capital City Belmopan
Population 321,115
Area 22,966 sq km
Main languages English, Spanish, Mayan, Garifuna (Carib), Creole

Haiti
Capital City Port-au-Prince
Population 9,719,932
Area 27,750 sq km
Main languages Creole, French

El Salvador
Capital City San Salvador
Population 6,071,774
Area 21,041 sq km
Main languages Spanish

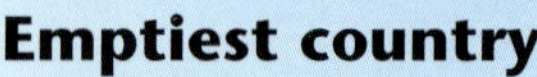

Emptiest country

The emptiest place in North America is Canada. It has lots of land and hardly any people. The most crowded place in North America is the Bahamas.

Honduras
Capital City Tegucigalpa
Population 8,143,564
Area 112,090 sq km
Main languages Spanish,
English and local languages

Dominican Republic
Capital City Santo Domingo
Population 9,956,648
Area 48,670 sq km
Main languages Spanish

Nicaragua
Capital City Managua
Population 5,666,301
Area 130,370 sq km
Main languages Spanish,
English and local languages

Jamaica
Capital City Kingston

Population 2,868,380
Area 10,991 sq km
Main languages English,
English patois

St Kitts and Nevis
Capital City Basseterre
Population 50,314
Area 261 sq km (St Kitts 168 sq
km; Nevis 93 sq km)
Main languages English

Antigua and Barbuda
Capital City Saint John's
Population 87,884
Area 442.6 sq km (Antigua 280
sq km; Barbuda 161 sq km)
Main languages English

Costa Rica
Capital City San Jose
Population 4,576,562
Area 51,100 sq km
Main languages Spanish,
English

The colourful Caribbean

The busy markets of the Caribbean are full of
colourful fruit and vegetables. Jamaica, Barbados
and the other islands are popular places to visit.

Panama
Capital City Panama City
Population 3,460,462
Area 75,420 sq km
Main languages Spanish,
English

Dominica
Capital City Roseau
Population 72,969
Area 751 sq km
Main languages English,
French patois

St Lucia
Capital City Castries
Population 161,557
Area 616 sq km
Main languages English,
French patois

**St Vincent and
the Grenadines**
Capital City Kingstown

Population 103,869
Area 389 sq km (St Vincent
344 sq km)
Main languages English

Barbados
Capital City Bridgetown
Population 286,705
Area 130 sq km
Area 430 sq km
Main languages English, Bajan

Grenada
Capital City Saint George's
Population 108,419
Area 344 sq km
Main languages English,
French patois

Trinidad and Tobago
Capital City Port-of-Spain
Population 1,227,505
Area 5,128 sq km
Main languages English

US DOLLARS

The United States dollar is the
official currency of the United
States of America. It is the
world's most important
currency, and it is used
everywhere for trading
gold and oil. Several
other countries also
use US dollars as
their official currency.

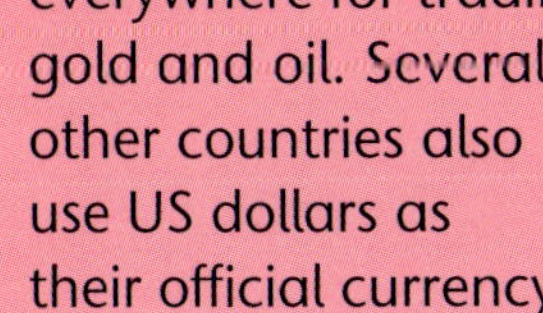

Africa

This is the second-biggest continent in the world. Africa has 55 countries and thousands of different languages. Africa also has the biggest desert in the world, called the Sahara. Hardly any people live in the desert because it is much too hot. Most of the people live near the coast or along the banks of rivers.

Biggest city

Africa's biggest city is Cairo, in Egypt. Almost 17 million people live here. Its nickname is 'city of 1,000 minarets'. You can see the tall minarets in this picture.

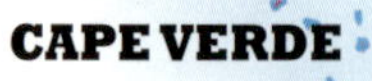

Biggest country

Sudan used to be the biggest single country in Africa, but now it has split into two countries, called Sudan and South Sudan. So now Algeria is Africa's biggest country!

ABOUT AFRICA

NUMBER OF COUNTRIES	55
SIZE	World's 2nd-largest continent
TOTAL AREA	30,221,532 sq kilometres
POPULATION	1.1 billion people
BIGGEST COUNTRY	Algeria – 2,381,741 square kilometres
SMALLEST COUNTRY	Seychelles – total area 451 square kilometres
BIGGEST CITY	Cairo, Egypt

High country

The highest country in the world is Lesotho, in South Africa. It is also one of the world's poorest countries. Most of the people living here are farmers.

Smallest country

The smallest country in Africa is the Republic of Seychelles. It is made up of 115 tropical islands in the Indian Ocean.

THE WOW!

Nobody is sure where the name 'Africa' is from. Some people think it comes from the word 'ufur', which means 'dust'. This could be true, because Africa is a dusty place!

FACTOR

Country-by-country facts

There are 55 countries in Africa and over 2,000 languages. Many of these languages belong to different tribes, so only a few people know how to speak them well. Africa has 42 official currencies. Many countries use US dollars and euros for trading abroad.

Morocco
Capital City Rabat
Population 31,968,361
Area 446,550 sq km
Main languages Arabic, Berber, French, Spanish

Algeria
Capital City Algiers
Population 34,994,937
Area 281,741 sq km
Main languages Arabic, French, Berber

Tunisia
Capital City Tunis
Population 10,629,186
Area 163,610 sq km
Main languages Arabic, French

Libya
Capital City Tripoli (Tarabulus)
Population 6,597,960
Area 1,759,540 sq km
Main languages Arabic

Egypt
Capital City Cairo
Population 82,079,636
Area 1,001,450 sq km
Main languages Arabic

Mauritania
Capital City Nouakchott
Population 3,281,634
Area 1,030,700 sq km
Main languages Arabic, French

Mali
Capital City Bamako
Population 14,159,904
Area 1,240,192 sq km
Main languages French, Bambara, Berber, Arabic

Niger
Capital City Niamey
Population 16,468,886
Area 1,267,000 sq km
Main languages French, Arabic, Hausa, Songhai

Chad
Capital City N'Djamena
Population 10,758,945
Area 1,284,000 sq km
Main languages French, Arabic

Sudan
Capital City Khartoum
Population 45,047,502
Area 2,505,813 sq km
Main languages Arabic, English

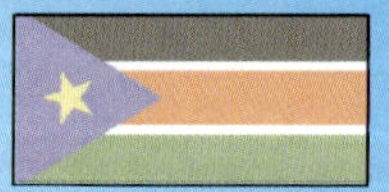

South Sudan
Capital City Juba
Population 8,260,490
Area 589,745 sq km (estimated)

Majestic mud

The Great Mosque at Djenne in Mali is the largest mud building in the world. It was built in 1907, and is made out of mud bricks covered with mud plaster. This type of mud building is called an 'adobe' building. People still build mud houses in many countries.

Main languages English,
Arabic (Juba Arabic)

Western Sahara
Capital City Laayoune
Population 507,160
Area 266,000 sq km
Main languages Hassaniya
Arabic, Moroccan Arabic

Burkina Faso
Capital City Ouagadougou
Population 16,751,455
Area 274,200 sq km
Main languages French and
local languages

Nigeria
Capital City Abuja
Population 155,215,573
Area 923,768 sq km
Main languages English,
Yoruba, Ibo, Hausa

Cameroon
Capital City Yaounde
Population 19,711,291
Area 475,440 sq km
Main languages French,
English, languages of Bantu,
Semi-Bantu and Sudanic groups

Central African Republic

Lively Morocco

This is the old city of
Marrakesh, in Morocco. It
is a lively, colourful place
and lots of tourists come
here. Morocco is very
close to Europe and it is a
cheap place to travel to.
People enjoy the
interesting crafts, food
and the warm climate.

Capital City Bangui
Population 4,950,027
Area 622,984 sq km
Main languages French,
Sangho (lingua franca)

Ethiopia
Capital City Addis Ababa
Population 90,873,739
Area 1,104,300 sq km
Main languages Amharic,
Oromo, Tigrinya, Somali

Eritrea
Capital City Asmara (Asmera)
Population 5,939,484
Area 117,600 sq km
Main languages Tigrinya,
Tigre, Arabic, English

Djibouti
Capital City Djibouti
Population 757,074
Area 23,200 sq km
Main languages French,
Arabic, Somali, Afar

Cape Verde
Capital City Praia
Population 516,100
Area 4,033 sq km
Main languages Portuguese,
Crioulo (a mixture of archaic
Portuguese and African words)

Senegal
Capital City Dakar
Population 12,643,799
Area 196,722 sq km
Main languages French, Wolof

Ghana
Capital City Accra
Population 24,791,073
Area 238,533 sq km
Main languages English,
African languages including
Akan, Ewe

Togo
Capital City Lome
Population 6,771,993
Area 56,785 sq km
Main languages French
and local languages

Benin
Capital City Porto-Novo
Population 9,325,032
Area 112,622 sq km
Main languages French, Fon,
Ge, Bariba, Yoruba, Dendi

Uganda
Capital City Kampala
Population 34,612,250
Area 241,038 sq km
Main languages English,
Swahili, Luganda, various Bantu
and Nilotic languages

Cattle farming

In Kenya and Tanzania cattle farming is very important. In these countries farmers such as the Maasai herd their cattle across the deserts and scrubland.

Kenya
Capital City Nairobi
Population 41,070,934
Area 580,367 sq km
Main languages Swahili, English

Somalia
Capital City Mogadishu
Population 9,925,640
Area 637,657 sq km
Main languages Somali, Arabic, Italian, English

Gambia
Capital City Banjul
Population 1,797,860
Area 11,295 sq km
Main languages English, Mandinka, Wolof, Fula

Guinea-Bissau
Capital City Bissau
Population 1,596,677
Area 36,125 sq km
Main languages Portuguese, Crioulo, African languages

Guinea
Capital City Conakry
Population 10,601,009
Area 245,857 sq km
Main languages French, Susu, Fulani, Mandingo

Rwanda
Capital City Kigali
Population 11,370,425
Area 26,338 sq km
Main languages Kinyarwanda, French, English, Swahili

Tanzania
Capital City Dodoma
Population 42,746,620
Area 947,300 sq km
Main languages English, Swahili

Seychelles
Capital City Victoria
Population 89,188
Area 455 sq km
Main languages English, French, Creole

Sierra Leone
Capital City Freetown
Population 5,363,669
Area 71,740 sq km
Main languages English, Krio (Creole language derived from English) and a range of African languages

Liberia
Capital City Monrovia
Population 3,786,764
Area 111,369 sq km
Main languages English and about 29 local African languages

Ivory Coast
Capital City Yamoussoukro
Population 21,504,162
Area 322,460 sq km
Main languages French and local languages

Democratic Republic of the Congo
Capital City Kinshasa
Area 71,712,867 sq km
Main languages French, Lingala, Kiswahili, Kikongo, Tshiluba

Burundi
Capital City Bujumbura
Population 10,216,190
Area 27,830 sq km
Main languages Kirundi, French, Swahili

Equatorial Guinea
Capital City Malabo
Population 668,225
Area 28,051 sq km
Main languages Spanish, French

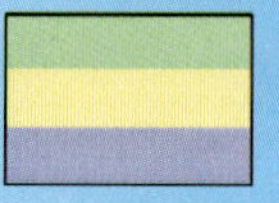

Gabon
Capital City Libreville
Population 1,576,665
Area 267,667 sq km
Main languages French, Bantu-group languages

Congo (Republic of the)
Capital City Brazzaville
Population 4,243,929
Area 342,000 sq km
Main languages French and local African languages

Malawi
Capital City Lilongwe
Population 15,879,252
Area 118,484 sq km
Main languages English, Chichewa

Mozambique
Capital City Maputo
Population 22,948,858
Area 799,380 sq km
Main languages Portuguese, Makua-Lomwe, Swahili and other local languages

Sao Tome and Principe
Capital City Sao Tome
Population 179,506
Area 964 sq km
Main languages Portuguese

Angola
Capital City Luanda
Population 13,338,541
Area 1,246,700 sq km
Main languages Portuguese, Umbundu, Kimbundu, Kikongo

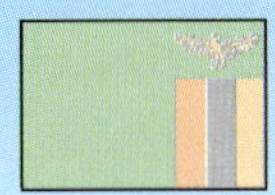

Zambia
Capital City Lusaka
Population 13,881,336
Area 752,618 sq km
Main languages English, Bemba, Lozi, Nyanja, Tonga

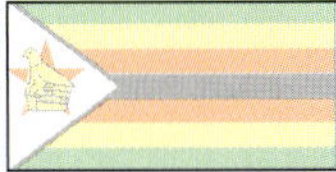

Zimbabwe
Capital City Harare
Population 12,084,304
Area 390,757 sq km
Main languages English, Shona, Sindebele

Madagascar
Capital City Antananarivo
Population 21,926,221
Area 587,041 sq km
Main languages Malagasy, French

Comoros
Capital City Moroni
Population 794,683
Area 2,235 sq km
Main languages Arabic, French, Comoran (a blend of Swahili and Arabic)

Namibia
Capital City Windhoek
Population 2,147,585
Area 824,292 sq km
Main languages English, Afrikaans, German, Oshivambo, Herero, Nama

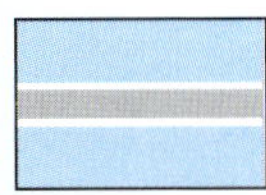

Botswana
Capital City Gaborone
Population 2,065,398
Area 581,730 sq km
Main languages English, Setswana

South Africa
Capital City Pretoria
Population 49,004,031
Area 1,219,090 sq km
Main languages 11 official languages including English, Afrikaans, Sesotho, Setswana, Xhosa and Zulu

Lesotho
Capital City Maseru
Population 1,924,886
Area 30,355 sq km
Main languages Sesotho, English

Swaziland
Capital City Mbabane
Population 1,370,424
Area 17,364 sq km
Main languages Swazi, English

Mauritius
Capital City Port Louis
Population 1,303,717
Area 2,040 sq km
Main languages English, Creole, French, Indian languages

SOUTH AFRICAN GOLD

More than one third of all the gold in the world has come from the gold mines in South Africa. The most common gold coin is the South African Kruggerand. This coin was first used in 1967 as a way to help ordinary people to own gold more easily. The coin is named after Paul Kruger, who was president of the old South African Republic. His picture is on one side of the coin. On the other side is a springbok, which is a symbol of South Africa.

Australasia and Oceania

The part of the world known as Australasia and Oceania contains 14 countries. The biggest country is Australia, and the smallest is Nauru. Many of the countries here are collections of little islands in the Pacific Ocean. A lot of the tiny islands have their own particular languages and customs. Most of the people here live close to the sea.

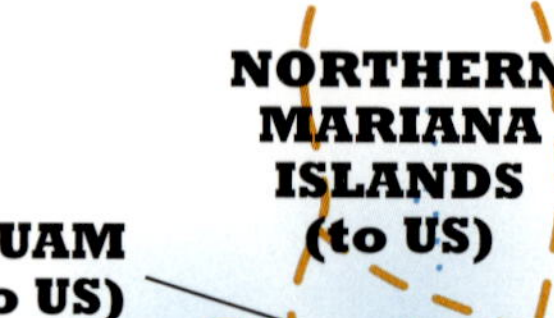

Biggest city

The largest city in this region is Sydney, in Australia. This beautiful city is small compared to many of the world's great cities. Only about 4.5 million people live in Sydney.

Biggest country

The biggest country and largest island in this region is Australia. There are big areas of scrubland outside most of the towns and cities. This is called 'the outback'.

Smallest country

This is a photograph of Nauru, the smallest island that is also a country. Once it was rich from selling guano (bird droppings) to make fertilizer. Now Nauru is poor because most of the guano has been sold.

THE WOW! FACTOR

Australia is one of the oldest islands in the world. It separated from the rest of the land billions of years ago. That is why it has so many unusual plants and animals!

ABOUT AUSTRALASIA AND OCEANIA

NUMBER OF COUNTRIES	14
SIZE	World's 7th-largest continent
TOTAL AREA	9,037,695 sq kilometres
POPULATION	38.9 million people
BIGGEST COUNTRY	Australia – 7,741,220 square kilometres
SMALLEST COUNTRY	Nauru – total area 21 square kilometres
BIGGEST CITY	Sydney, Australia

Country-by-country facts

Most of the people here speak English, but there are also thousands of other languages. There are hundreds of religions and cultures too. About half of the countries do not have their own currencies. Instead, they use the US, Australian or New Zealand dollar.

Marshall Islands
Capital City Majuro
Population 67,182
Area 181 sq km
Main languages Marshallese, English

Palau
Capital City Ngerulmud (Melekeok)
Population 20,956
Area 459 sq km
Main languages Palauan, English

Micronesia
Capital City Palikir
Population 106,836
Area 702 sq km
Main languages English, Trukese, Pohnpeian, Yapese, Kosrean

Nauru
Capital City Yaren (unofficial)
Population 9,322
Area 21 sq km
Main languages Nauruan, English

Kiribati
Capital City Tarawa
Population 100,743
Area 811 sq km
Main languages English, Gilbertese

Papua New Guinea
Capital City Port Moresby
Population 6,187,591
Area 462,840 sq km
Main languages English, Tok Pisin, Hiri Motu

Solomon Islands
Capital City Honiara
Population 571,890
Area 28,896 sq km
Main languages English, Melanese

Tuvalu
Capital City Fanafuti
Population 10,544
Area 26 sq km
Main languages Tuvaluan, English

Big island

New Guinea is the world's second-biggest island. The country of Papua New Guinea takes up half of this island. There are over 820 languages in Papua New Guinea. A lot of people here live in tribal groups in villages, like their ancestors did hundreds of years ago. These men from Papua New Guinea are wearing traditional headdresses.

Fiji islands

Only a tiny part of the country of Fiji is made up of land. The rest of it is sea. Fiji has over 300 islands and lots of tiny islands called islets. Only about one-third of the islands have people living on them.

This carving from New Zealand is called a 'tiki'.

Samoa
Capital City Apia
Population 193,161
Area 2,831 sq km
Main languages Samoan, English

Fiji
Capital City Suva
Population 883,125
Area 18,274 sq km
Main languages English, Fijian, Hindi

Australia
Capital City Canberra
Population 21,766,711
Area 7,741,220 sq km
Main languages English

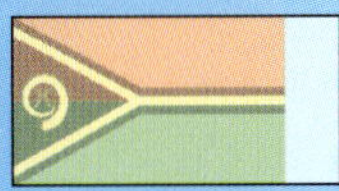

Vanuatu
Capital City Port-Vila
Population 224,564
Area 12,189 sq km
Main languages Bislama, French, English

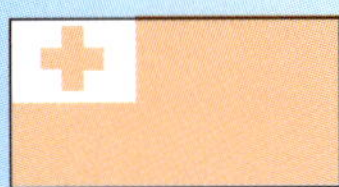

Tonga
Capital City Nuku'alofa
Population 105,916
Area 747 sq km
Main languages Tongan, English

New Zealand
Capital City Wellington
Population 4,290,347
Area 267,710 sq km
Main languages English, Maori

NEW ZEALAND

The beautiful country of New Zealand was one of the last places on Earth to be discovered by humans. A lot of it is still covered in forest. Some of the world's oldest trees, called kauris, still grow here. New Zealand is famous for its sheep farming, wool and leather, and for growing apples and pears, which are exported to Europe.

Sheep grazing on the rich pastures of New Zealand

South America

This is the fourth-largest continent in the world. South America has 12 countries. The biggest country is Brazil and the smallest is Suriname. Brazil takes up almost half of all the land in South America. It has more people than any of the other countries. Lots of Europeans moved here about 500 years ago and most people speak Spanish or Portuguese.

Biggest forest

Earth's largest rainforest is in South America. More than half of the rainforest is in Brazil. It also covers land that belongs to eight other countries. Brazil has the huge River Amazon too. This is the largest river on Earth!

Smallest country

Suriname is the smallest country in South America. It is close to the Equator so it has a very hot tropical climate. Most of the people speak several languages, including Dutch.

Longest country

Chile is the world's longest country. In the north are the high Andes mountains, which run all the way down South America. This is the biggest range of mountains on Earth.

Biggest city

The huge, modern Brazilian city of Sao Paulo is the largest city in South America. Sao Paulo now has a population of more than 11 million people.

ABOUT SOUTH AMERICA

NUMBER OF COUNTRIES	12
SIZE	World's 4th-largest continent
TOTAL AREA	17,840.000sq kilometres
POPULATION	392.5 million people
BIGGEST COUNTRY	Brazil – 8,514,877 square kilometres
SMALLEST COUNTRY	Suriname – total area 163,820 square kilometres
BIGGEST CITY	Sao Paulo, Brazil

Country-by-country facts

There are 12 countries in South America and about 350 languages are spoken. The most widely spoken languages are Portuguese and Spanish. There are 13 currencies in South America, including the euro, which is used in French Guiana.

Colombia
Capital City Bogota
Population 44,725,543
Area 1,138,910 sq km
Main languages Spanish

Venezuela
Capital City Caracas
Population 27,635,743
Area 912,050 sq km
Main languages Spanish and local languages

Guyana
Capital City Georgetown
Population 744,768
Area 214,969 sq km
Main languages English, Creole, Hindi, Urdu and local languages

Suriname
Capital City Paramaribo
Population 491,989
Area 163,820 sq km
Main languages Dutch, English, Sranang Tongo, Hindi, Javanese

Ecuador
Capital City Quito
Population 15,007,343
Area 283,561 sq km
Main languages Spanish, local languages

Peru
Capital City Lima
Population 29,248,943
Area 1,285,216 sq km
Main languages Spanish, Quechua, Aymara

Brazil
Capital City Brasilia
Population 203,429,773
Area 8,514,877 sq km
Main languages Portuguese

Bolivia
Capital City La Paz and Sucre
Population 10,118,683
Area 1,098,581 sq km
Main languages Spanish, Quechua, Aymara, Guarani

Busy Bolivia

The population of Bolivia includes Amerindians, Asians, Mestizos, Europeans and Africans. Most of the people speak Spanish, but there are also over 35 local languages.

A country called Colombia

Columbia is named after the famous explorer Christopher Columbus, although he never actually visited here. It was his companion, Alonso de Ojeda, who was the first European to land here, in 1499.

Wealthy capital

Santiago is the capital of Chile. This modern city has become a rich, important trading place in the last 50 years. It has smart offices and shopping malls, and attractive areas where people can live.

Colourful houses

The capital of Argentina is Buenos Aires. Some of the older houses are painted in jolly colours. The city has grown much larger in the last 100 years. Over 15 million people live here now!

Paraguay
Capital City Asuncion
Population 6,459,058
Area 406,752 sq km
Main languages Spanish, Guarani

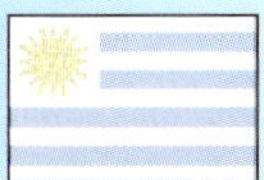

Uruguay
Capital City Montevideo
Population 3,308,535
Area 176,215 sq km
Main languages Spanish, Portunol, Brazilero

Chile
Capital City Santiago
Population 16,888,760
Area 756,102 sq km
Main languages Spanish

Argentina
Capital City Buenos Aires
Population 41,769,726
Area 2,780,400 sq km
Main languages Spanish

RIO CARNIVAL

Many Catholic countries around the world have a carnival every year at the beginning of Lent. This is 40 days before Easter. The biggest and most famous of these carnivals is in Brazil. The celebrations carry on through the day and night in every town and city. The country stops completely for almost a week for the party!

Members of a dance troupe parading through the streets

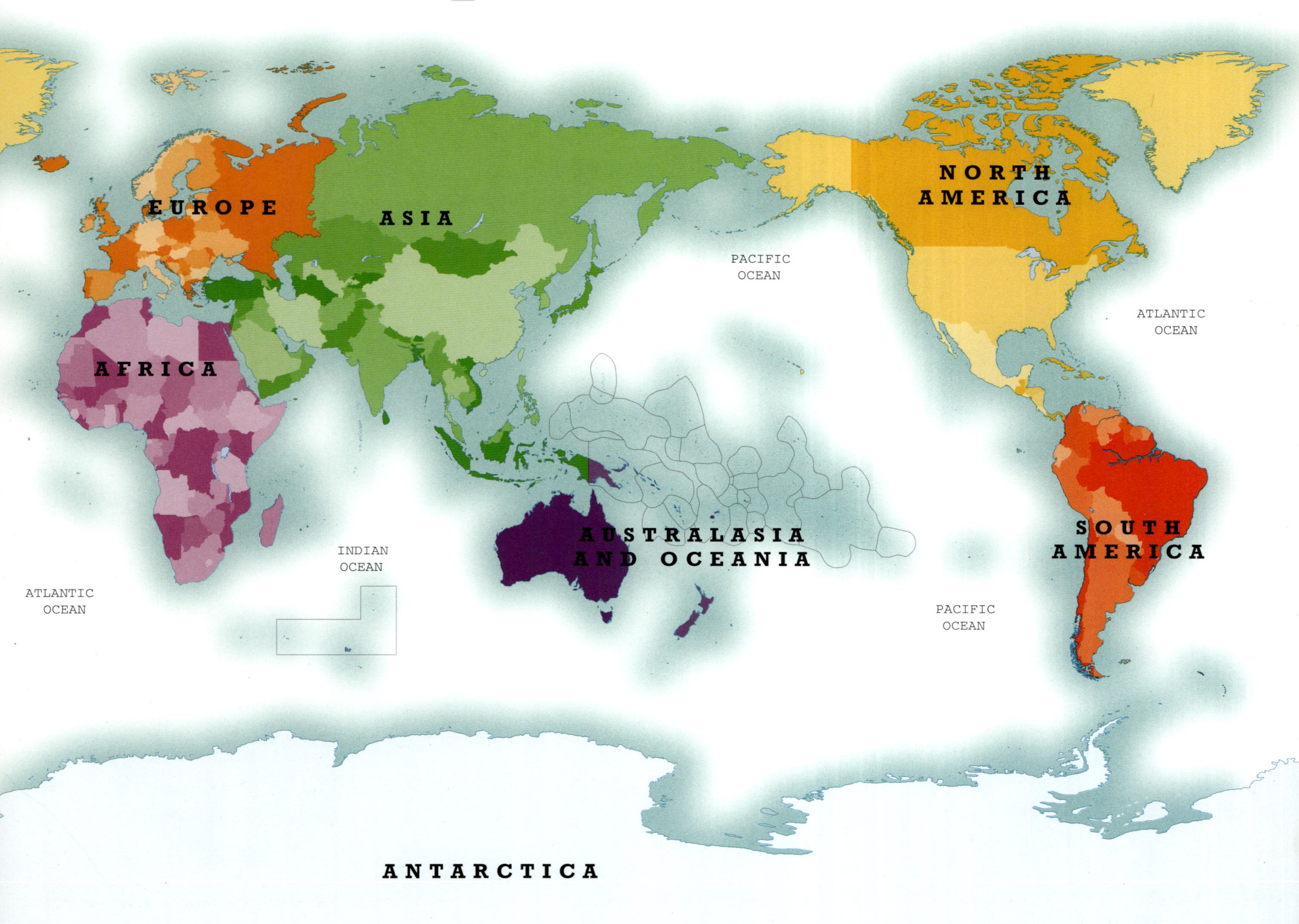

Map of the world
EUROPE
ASIA
NORTH AMERICA
PACIFIC OCEAN
ATLANTIC OCEAN
AFRICA
ATLANTIC OCEAN
INDIAN OCEAN
AUSTRALASIA AND OCEANIA
SOUTH AMERICA
PACIFIC OCEAN
ANTARCTICA

Europe
Asia

Asia
Africa

North America
South America

South America

Australasia and
Oceania

Have fun with these extra stickers!